ART NOUVEAU POSTCARDS

The Posterists' Postcards

by Alain Weill

Images Graphiques
New York

Translated from the French
by Bernard Jacobson.

IMAGES GRAPHIQUES, INC.
37 Riverside Drive
New York, New York 10023

Library of Congress Catalog Card Number: 77–94470

ISBN (Softcover) 0–89545–015–1
ISBN (Hardcover) 0–89545–014–3

First Printing, November 1977

Printed in the United States of America

THE POSTCARD LIBRARY

The main purpose of this book is to be a volume of pictures: pictures which at the turn of the century were in great demand by aficionados of the postcard. It is quite evident that by reproducing a few dozen postcards we have never had the ambitious task of presenting a history of the illustrated card. In a field where systematic research has hardly begun, such study still has to be written and, when it is, it shall require several large volumes. Our selection, nevertheless, corresponds to a number of predetermined criteria.

We have focused our attention on purely decorative postcards, leaving out advertising cards. Other than the esthetic choice it represents, it seemed to us that it would be difficult for the reader (except in a few cases, such as the French Cinos series) to discern if the document reproduced would be a poster, a hand bill, or a card. Another reason is that those cards, whose function it was to advertise, are of a different spirit and graphic design than the purely decorative cards which make up this work.

Furthermore, we have intended, despite the limited number of pages at our disposal, to present as broad a range as possible of the world production at the beginning of the century. The countries which are not represented (as in the case of the United States) are those for which we were unable to locate items which seemed to harmonize with the concept of this offering.

We have given this first volume in The Postcard Library the title "Art Nouveau Postcards." Though a large number of the cards reproduced belong to a floral art, that is to the narrowest idea of the words "art nouveau," Art Nouveau in this case should be considered in its broadest meaning, namely, as a reaction against academism, the one thing which all the artists represented here have in common.

Finally, by means of our subtitle, we have tried to indicate (without deliberately expressing the slightest preference!) the link which existed at the time between two graphic modes of expression, the poster and the postcard, both of which were, simultaneously, in considerable vogue. Indeed, many of the cards in this album have been designed by illustrators who regularly devoted themselves to the poster.

We are aware of the inevitable subjectivity of our choices, and a thousand other selections would have been possible. This then is the wonderful (and awesome) privilege of putting together such a collection—it is the privilege and joy that collectors experience daily. We can only hope that the reader will share in that spirit with us.

INTRODUCTION

"Correspondence cards", as they were called then, were first introduced in Austria on October 1st, 1869. In the years that followed they made their appearance in many other countries: July 1st, 1870 in Germany; in 1871 in England, Belgium and Switzerland; then in Russia and in France in 1872; in the United States and in Spain in 1873; in Italy in 1874, the year the Bern Postal Treaty admitted them in international service. Their success was considerable and instant. In Berlin, on the first day they were put on the market, 45,468 cards were mailed, and in two months two million were mailed in Germany alone. In May of 1873, the first month the postcard was in use in the United States, 31 million cards were sold.

Moreover, this new medium of correspondence was at its inception only a card without any illustration: the picture appeared only little by little. Since the war of 1870, two pioneers, Schwarz in Germany and Besnardeau in France, printed cards with patriotic and military motifs: it was only a hesitant beginning, even before the process was officially recognized. It was only progressively, and often thanks to advertising, that illustration developed. The role of the German-speaking countries was preponderant in this development. As early as 1875 Schwarz put twenty-five humorous cards on the market; he was soon imitated by other publishers, and from that point on the movement conquered the world.

The golden age of the postcard spans the first twenty years of our century. In 1899, production reached 88 million in Germany, 14 million in Great Britain, 12 million in Belgium and 8 million in France. Of course, most of these were photographic cards. Among the drawn cards (probably one tenth of the production) the "gruss", "voeux" and other greetings constituted a large majority. The subject of this book is the small portion of cards with artistic pretensions.

These decorative postcards are directly linked to the prodigious revival of print at the end of the 19th century. The print, until then confined to the reproduction of classical tableaux, became the preferred instrument of a spirited generation of young artists who, in reaction to Academism fought for a new art, "art nouveau", which should not be considered synonymous with floral art but as an art in opposition to official art. Lithography, with recent improvements which made it possible to produce a great number of plates, in color and at low cost, arrived in the nick of time to serve this purpose.

But the novelty does not lie only in this renewal of creativity. The traditional realm of the print was itself considerably broadened. Two great discoverers, the brothers Goncourt, had launched the vogue of collecting handbills, menus and other ephemera at the end of the 18th century. This domain of the "small print," *(la petite estampe)*, as De Crauzat called it, participated in a new approach to art. With Roger Marx, who protested against "a blind, detestable bias in favor of abstract creations which has shrunk the field of art and rendered the notion of art inseparable from the idea of luxury and high-brow culture," the fight was joined to return to the decorative arts—considered as minor or inferior—the essential place they deserved, and which they had occupied during the Middle-Ages.

The triumph of this social art, the poster, rapidly covered the walls and became fashionable. "Now it is the poster that brings joy to the print collector," wrote Henri Beraldi. From the largest to the smallest format, this concern to introduce art into daily life predominated. Roger Marx was pleading for a new effort in the design of postage stamps where "the smallness of the format represents only an illusory obstacle to inspiration." This remark was equally valid for the postcard which, just as the poster, became the success of the day. Although they are of a different format, these two types of prints have in common the power to bring art to the masses.

Leonetto Cappiello, the father of the modern poster, was quite aware of this when he stated: "Not only do I find it charming, to correspond by means of the illustrated card, but also interesting because if we know how to take advantage of it, it may become a very useful tool to reveal art to the masses." It is therefore not surprising, from our point of view, that artists who were interested in the poster also liked to express themselves with the postcard. Steinlen, Villon or Mucha in France, Beardsley or Hassal in England, Hohenstein, Mataloni and Metlicovitz in Italy, Combaz or Meunier in Belgium as well as Kokoschka or Koloman Moser in Vienna, Casas or Utrillo in Barcelona are here, among others, to prove the point.

Although involved in a more political struggle, the caricaturists who worked side by side with these artists for avantgarde magazines such as *Simplicissimus* or *Jugend* in the German-speaking countries, *L'Assiette au beurre* or *Le Rire* in France, also tried their hand at the postcard. Other elements are also evidence of the indivisible links which united print, postcard and poster. The magazines *La Plume* in Paris and *The Poster* in London opened their columns to the postcard.

From 1895 to 1900 the Chaix printing firm published *The Masters of the Poster; The Masters of the Postcard* appeared in 1899; and *The Collection of One Hundred*—a collection of cards published by Greningaire from 1901 on—had more than the title in common with the "Salon of the One Hundred" *(Salon des Cent)* where artists exhibited Art Nouveau works and where in 1901 the first exhibition of postcards in Paris was organized.

Recorded, classified and shown as models to follow, these creations influenced a slew of disciples. Avant-garde publishers—like Dietrich in Brussels, Philipp & Kramer in Vienna or Ricordi in Milan and Raphael Tuck in London—the giants of the postcard—concurrently issued many series of art postcards. For the most part they used minor masters, clumsy interpreters of that which is most easily imitated in Art Nouveau: the floral style. With a few exceptions (i.e., Eva Daniell) their considerable production is one of a great awkwardness and bad taste.

It seemed to us important to place the artistic postcard in the context that made for its development, to remind us of its relationship to the poster and the movement of which both media were an integral part. These original works bear witness to a time when people dared believe in an art that was truly accessible to the public.

—Alain Weill
Paris
October, 1977

AUTHOR'S ACKNOWLEDGMENTS

I would like to thank here all those who directly or indirectly helped with my arduous task.

By showing me the "Collection of the One Hundred", my friend Bourgeron spurred my resolve to write this book. Nicolas Rémon, with his customary kindness and urbanity, gave me access to his library and collection. André Gontier did the same and let me take advantage of his vast scholarship. I thank them for it wholeheartedly, as well as François Derain who entrusted me with valuable documentation.

This book owes a lot to the pleasant as well as enriching conversations I had in New York with Asa Pieratt who lent us several items from his collection for this album.

I am grateful also to George Theofiles for details he may have given me over a bottle of Beaujolais (which for some mysterious reason they refused to serve chilled).

Thanks to Georges Philippenko with whom the book provided an opportunity to lunch pleasantly, to Hervé Chayette who read the text and found it interesting, to Gilles Ghez (to whom he mentioned it, and who told me) to Janique Ladouar—to whom I transmitted this judgment—for believing it.

Thanks to my colleagues Andrée Benchetrit, Ralph Delval, Jean-Michel Goutier and Christophe Zagrodzski for having been there, on my side. A special mention must be made of Réjane Bargiel without whom nothing is possible.

Thanks to Helen Garfinkle, and Joan Saranga, from Images Graphiques who patiently listened to the nonsense and the puns with which I stud my creative work.

Thanks to the Rennerts who go out of their way to please me and bear with a smile my most outlandish whims.

Finally, thanks to Geneviève Picon for always encouraging me in my endeavors.

PUBLISHER'S ACKNOWLEDGMENTS

All postcards in this volume are reproduced in their original size and color. All are from the collection of the Musée des Arts Décoratifs, Paris, with the exception of the following numbers which are from the collection of Mr. Asa Pieratt: 27–38, 73–76, 79, 105, 111–116, 119–122. To the administration of the Musée des Arts Décoratifs and to Mr. Asa Pieratt, our deepest appreciation for making their splendid collection available to us. Since all reproductions in this volume are directly made from the original postcards, our gratitude also for the work of two fine photographers, Mr. Ralph Delval in Paris and Mr. Martin Jackson in New York. Color separations were carefully handled by Mr. Kanae Akiyama of Daiichi Seihan, ably assisted by Mr. Tomeji Maruyama. Design and lay-out was under the supervision of Mr. Harry Chester, with assistance of Mr. Alexander Soma of his staff. Typography was handled in timely fashion by Precision Typoraphers. The entire production was under the capable management of the staff of Federated Graphics Companies, and we are especially indebted to Mr. Herbert Scharer of their New York office and Mr. John D. Netsel at the Rhode Island plant. The staff of Images Graphiques proved most helpful and special thanks are due to Ms. Helen Garfinkle, Mr. Chester Collins, and Mr. Stu Solow.

—The Publisher

BIBLIOGRAPHY

The postcard is a domain that is just being rediscovered. Although many thematic studies, such as this one, have recently been published, so far no comprehensive work exists. In the meantime I wholeheartedly recommend the following: Ado Kirou's *L'âge d'or de la carte postale* (The Golden Age of the Postcard) (Balland: Paris, 1966) and *L'album de cartes postales—reflet de la Belle époque* (The Album of Postcards—a Reflection of the Belle Epoque) by A. Jakovsky and C. Lauterbach (Flammarion: Paris); both of these books include an excellent bibliography. And finally, the cartophileś vademecum, Joëlle and Gerard Neudin's *L'Argus international des cartes postales* which, since 1973, has provided the enthusiasts with invaluable information.

I am indebted to my friend Asa Pieratt for calling my attention to two general reference works on the subject which are available to English-speaking readers of this volume: George and Dorothy Miller's *Picture Postcards in the United States, 1893–1918* (Clarkson Potter: New York, 1976) and Marian Klamkin's *Picture Postcards* (Dodd, Mead & Co: New York, 1974).

1–6. THÉOPHILE ALEXANDRE STEINLEN (1859–1923).

Steinlen came from Switzerland and in 1878 he settled in Paris. In Montmartre he befriended Willette who introduced him to the circle of the Chat Noir and the great Aristide Bruant. He contributed to many journals, including the *Chat Noir*, *Gil Blas* and *Le Mirliton* (in which he illustrated Bruant's songs) as well as to *Le Rire* and *L'Assiette au Beurre*. He illustrated numerous works (Artistide Bruant's *Dans la rue*, Delmet's songs and also works by Jean Richepin, Jehan Rictus, Félicien Champsaur and Anatole France). He was a great posterist and we are indebted to him for many fine examples of this medium: Yvette Guilbert and the Ambassadeurs (1894), the pure milk of the Vingeanne (1894), Le Chat Noir (1896), Verneau's "La Rue" (1896), La Traite des Blanches ("White Slavery", 1899), Cocorico (1899), and L'Assomoir (1900), to name only a few of these classics.

Naturally, he was interested in the postcard, and his eminent position in the field entitled him to the number three ranking in the series of the "One Hundred". For this series he again treated his favorite subjects—for the postcards of the Union Artistique (series 101) he went back to a familiar subject, Bruant's songs, and in 1902, for Greningaire, he produced a series of ten colored cards which have as a theme the life of young working women. Six of these cards are reproduced in this album. Here we find the favorite scenes of this dyed-in-the-wool socialist, lover of the people of Paris whom he painted so admirably in his work. The young working girls, easy prey of a city where money, embodied by enterprising old men or the charms of the young pimps, seem to push them irremediably towards a streetwalker's life. Harassed in a shop or mistreated in a household, with their poor quality skirts and their skimpy bodices, their hair in a bun over their head, they search for love and a little happiness on this road full of traps. Steinlen depicts them the way Aristide Bruant sang about them or Charles Louis Philippe described them in *Bubu de Montparnasse*.

7. ABEL FAIVRE (1867–1945).

A student of Jean-Baptiste Poncet in Lyon, Faivre went to Paris to continue his studies in the studio of Benjamin Constant. In addition to being a painter, he was a caricaturist of the first order. He displayed his savage satire in *Le Rire* and *L'Assiette au beurre* for which he created an exceptionally virulent issue devoted to physicians.

In his drawings, young women, old maids and lewd sexagenarians embody human baseness in life situations.

He was an occasional posterist and an eminent member of the Society of Humorists.

For the Henri Monnier Gala he executed the postcard shown here, on which, with his usual vigor, he drew a red-faced bourgeois, inflated with his own importance, impatiently waving his hat.

8. LUBIN DE BEAUVAIS.

Best known as an illustrator of books for young people, Lubin de Beauvais was also a regular member of the Society of Humorists: He took part in the Humorists' Exposition in Copenhagen (1909) and in Paris' "Salon des Humoristes".

On the subject of the Henri Monnier Ball, he produced two postcards of equal quality. The one we reproduce here—an elegant young lady thumbing her nose at a stodgy bourgeois who has just offered her a hat—is illustrative, as is the rest of the series, of the response the propertied classes, so smug about their triumphant prosperity and their conventional values, would elicit from those they could not (for lack of other means) please (that is to say use) except with money.

9. CHARLES LÉANDRE (1862–1934).

Charles Léandre, designer, painter, sculptor and engraver was one of the most influential members of the Society of Humorists which he founded, together with Louis Morin. It was he who, at the Henri Monnier Gala held on June 1st, 1904 for the benefit of the humorists' welfare fund, had the privilege of immortalizing Monsieur Prudhomme (the pompous bourgeois) in The Ceremony of the Triumph and Coronation of Monsieur Joseph Prudhomme. This eminent position probably entitled him to the number seven spot in the Collection of One Hundred. In this drawing, as well as all those for *La Vie Moderne*, *La Grosse Caisse*, *Le Chat Noir*, or *Le Rire* he offers us "a detailed composition where human baseness assumes a character of profound bitterness," according to Francis Carco. Just as all his colleagues, Charles Léandre illustrated books and also left a good number of posters for the theater or for exhibits (Société des peintres lithographes, 1897; Cantomimes de Xavier Privas, 1899; Le Vieux Marcheur, "The Old Walker," 1899; Le Roi de Rome, "The King of Rome," 1899; Le Mariage, 1900; and others.)

This card—as well as numbers 18, 22, 25, 26, 39, 40—belongs to the "Collection of One Hundred." They are mostly original compositions tinted by the publisher, Gréningaire. They were issued in booklets of ten from November 1901 on; to date we have a record of 98 of these cards. The last ones are not numbered, probably because of publishing difficulties. These cards represent the most important French effort in the realm of the illustrated postcard.

10. PAUL IRIBE (1883–1935).

An eclectic personality, Paul Iribe exercised his many talents during the first 35 years of the century, right up to his death. He was above all known as a master of the Art Deco style. Jacques Doucet picked him to furnish his new apartment, 46 Avenue du Bois. In the winter of 1914–15 he went to the United States and worked for the theater and cinema with Cecil B. de Mille. Upon his return to France in 1930, he designed jewelry for Miss Chanel. Iribe's style was for a long time influenced by the fluid form of the "modern style" and manifests itself in a refined elegance and comfort. He liked opulent materials, color contrast, ornaments: the most famous is the "Iribe rose". His collaboration with Poiret has remained famous because of the publication of "The Things of Paul Poiret As Seen by Paul Iribe." His drawings for *Le Bleu, Le Blanc,* and *Le Rouge,* ("The Blue," "The White" and "The Red"), three albums published by Vins Nicolas (Nicolas Wines) are three masterpieces among the many works which he illustrated. People have forgotten that he had a talent for satire which he developed all during his career: a contributor to *Le Rire, Au Canard sauvage* and *Le Cri de Paris,* he published from 1914 to 1918 the magazine *Le mot* with participation of Dufy, Lhote, Cocteau and Sem. In this journal, as well as in *La baïonnette* and later in *Le témoin,* which he edited from 1933 until 1935, he drew caricatures of extreme patriotic violence.

His card for the Henri Monnier Gala, although a work from his youth, is already a work of extreme vigor and violence, a variation on the theme of the "Père la pudeur" (Father Modesty) (cf. Villon). He has the undressed model at a student ball (probably the Quat 'z' arts) say that Mimi Pinson has only a cap. This makes the decorated old man—probably a lover of classical nudes as long as their sex is hidden by a garment or an angel—and an old watcher of the feminine calf, at a time when every square inch of bare flesh had its meaning, as angry as he is flabbergasted.

11–14. JACQUES VILLON (1875–1963).

Jacques Villon is, of course, mainly known as a painter and the role he played, side by side with Delaunay, Braque and Juan Gris, in the development of Cubism.

Gaston Duchamp, Marcel Duchamp's brother, arrived in Paris in 1895 to study law. He was much more interested in drawing than in law and to avoid his bourgeois family's disapproval he changed his name: "I chose Villon on account of the poet and Jack on account of Alphonse Daudet's novel *Jack.*" Somewhat later he gallicized his name to Jacques Villon, and this signature appeared in the *Courrier Francais,* the second *Chat Noir, L'Assiette au Beurre, Le Rire, La Lanterne,* and *Le Quartier Latin.* He contributed many satiric drawings to these journals. Villon, as well as all the illustrators of the period, passionately devoted himself to lithography, creating prints and posters: La guinguette fleurie ("Roadside Inn with Flowers,"(1898), "Le Grillon" (1899), "L'Anti-Bélier" (1898), etc. Connected with the Montmartre art circles—the influence of Lautrec (whom he knew) on his work was perceptible at the time —he contributed regularly to humor journals, and it seems only normal that he was asked to make some cards for the Henri Monnier Gala.

We are reproducing four of the eight cards we know he created. They are of a superb quality: the drawing is animated, smart, full of life and movement, rendered even more caustic by strokes of color which the lithography shows to great advantage. In two of the cards a woman is confronted by a man. In one, the man is taken aback by the sight of an undressed seductress; in the other, a stern man is heaping insults upon a woman who, in response, covers her ears with her hands. The name Bérenger, printed on the newspapers, allows us to assume that the grouser we are dealing with here is the famous Senator Bérenger, the patron of modesty, president of the Society Against Street Licentiousness, who won fame in a court case he initiated following the first ball of the École des Beaux-Arts, the Bal des Quat 'z' arts, where some models bared too much flesh for his liking. From then on the patron of modesty became the artists' favorite target and became entitled, at the time of the 1897 ball, to his own bust at the entrance of the École des Beaux-Arts. This bust was paired with one of a charming bare-breasted woman. It was also due to Bérenger's intervention in 1904 that certain postcards had to be "dressed again" because he found them to be indecent.

15. GEORGES REDON (1869–1943).

Georges Redon's career was split between painting (he exhibited each year at the *Salon d'automne)* and illustration. He was also a member of the Society of Humorists and left us many illustrations, theater posters (Lyane de Pougy at the Casino de Paris, Eldorado, qu 'est-ce qui se passe? ("What Is Going On?", 1905) and a postcard for the Henri Monnier Gala, shown here, where he presented his version of the stupid bourgeois, triumphant and lascivious. Redon's lithographic talent is quite evident from this postcard.

16. CHARLES EMILE CARLÈGLE (1877–1940).

In the first half of his life Carlègle was a prolific caricaturist, a member of the Society of Humorists. He abandoned this activity to devote himself to the illustration of classical texts: Pierre Louys' *King Pausole* and then La Fontaine, Virgil, Ronsard, Verlaine, Courteline, Paul Fort, Pascal, Montherlant, Valéry, etc . . . His card for the Henri Monnier Gala, using modern workmanship and a comic strip style, shows Mister Prudhomme in a rustic scene, with his wife, his child—rigged out in a soldier's uniform—his dog and his inseparable umbrella . . . We are at once aware of the ludicrousness of this pompous figure.

17. ABEL TRUCHET (1857–1918).

A student of Benjamin Constant, Truchet was a painter of landscapes and Parisian scenes in the impressionistic manner. He also participated in the "Salon des Humoristes". He was a lithographer and a posterist of talent: he drew the Cabaret des Quat'z arts (1894), The Horse Shoe English and American Bar (1896), Cyclistes buvez le vin blanc de Pouilly ("Cyclists Drink the White Wine of Pouilly," 1896), and one of the first cinema posters showing two women with hats watching on a screen "The Arrival of a Train in the Sète Railway Station", one of the Lumière Brothers' first films.

18. SEM (1863–1934).

The son of a grocer from Perigueux, Sem (whose real name was Serge Goursat) lived in Bordeaux and Marseilles—where he met Cappiello who influenced his style—and finally arrived in Paris in 1900. He became well known at the race tracks and in fashionable restaurants. In June of that same year he published his first album which very much amused the Parisian social set. From that time on he became known for his talent as a caricaturist as well as for his niggardliness. Until his death he published albums loaded with acutely discerning portraits of members of Parisian high society, whether in Deauville or at Maxim's. As Baron Fouquier noted: "We should be grateful to him for he left us a lively recollection of a society and an era which, with the passing of time, will be of real value to those interested in the subject." In addition to his caricatures he produced a number of posters (Deauville, Polin, Footit) making generous use of large tinted surfaces, and this card of the Collection of One Hundred (#51) which presents one of his favored scenes: a great restaurant, two floozies, a dandy and the indispensable staff, of the establishment.

19–20. HENRI BOUTET (1851–1920).

Sea bathing became fashionable at the end of the last century, the very same period which became the heyday of the postcard. It became a pretext for many jokes and bawdy pranks, and we could devote an entire album to the subject.

We are grateful to Henri Boutet for the two postcards which represent the vogue in this book; they are smartly designed and show in detail the bathing suits of the day as well as the prank of the pinching crab.

Illustrator, regular contributor to humor and satirical magazines, Boutet was one of the best painters of the "Parisian woman", often in the bawdy scenes which were so much a part of the mood of the times. In 1895 he executed a charming poster for an exposition of his work at the "Salon des Cent".

21. PAUL HELLEU (1859–1927).

Helleu was one of the most popular painters of feminine charm and frivolity at the end of the century. An important person in Parisian society, he was the preferred painter of the Belle Epoque's elegant society. He left a gallery of portraits. He was also an engraver and lithographer. Many black and white cards were printed which reproduced the master's elegant feminine silhouettes.

22. JULES CHÉRET (1836–1932).

Inventor of the modern color, pictorial poster, Jules Chéret produced almost one thousand posters between 1866 and 1900. The living embodiment of this art, decorated and honored, he then decided to devote himself to paintings and frescoes. His contribution to the postcard is an exception. The handbills, menus, as well as invitations (for instance, the one for the Bal des Quat 'z arts), which he designed are legion. He honored the "Collection of One Hundred" by contributing the only non-advertising item which he ever produced in this size. It represents Colombine, a character of the theater, touched up with white chalk the way he liked to draw her, in the manner of the French painters of the 18th century.

23. "M. FELIN".

It seems to us that the signature on this card reads "M. Felin." That doesn't tell us anything about the author. However, the card is a beautiful, very French lithograph of a woman's face. The striped, vividly yellow background skillfully brings the face into relief.

24. JULES ALEXANDRE GRÜN (1868–1934).

Grün did not have to overstrain to find a subject for his card for the Henri Monnier Gala: he simply put Monsieur Prudhomme (the pompous bourgeois) in the place of the numerous bitter old men surrounded by women of easy virtue, with their well displayed cleavage, who people his posters for the cabarets of Montmartre (Au Violin, Le Tréteau de Tabarin, La Pepinière, La Cigale, La Scala, etc . . .). He skillfully used the black background to describe the men's formal attire or to represent a policeman's uniform. He liked his characters to extend beyond the frame of the picture the way he did in this postcard. His complementary color was generally the red in which he draped the women.

A Montmartre type par excellence, Grün contributed his work to journals such as *La caricature*, *Le Fin de Siècle*, or *Le Courrier français*. He also illustrated Xanroff's *Chansons sans gêne* and his *Chansons à rire* as well as *Le guide de l'étranger à Montmartre ("The Foreigner's Guide to Montmartre") and other works of this kind*.

Grün's bald head and Assyrian beard left Montmartre, rue des Abbesses, and its pleasures for the rue Berthier after his marriage to a talented concert artist, Miss Toutain; he then devoted himself to official art and was, of course, given all the official honors.

25. G. CONRAD.

As is the case with so many other cards in the "Collection of One Hundred," not much is known about the artist, here G. Conrad. Conrad did illustrate some books in the 1920's and 1930's but little more can be gathered about his career. His card is a curious mixture of decorative Art Nouveau elements and very Parisian illustration. His bold strokes frame a little woman that, with the exception of the clothing frills, could have been drawn by Boutet or Guillaume. This freshly colored composition is a visual delight.

26. CARAN D'ACHE (1859–1909).

It is undoubtedly his birth in Moscow that led Emmanuel Poiré to choose the alias Caran d'Ache, which means "pencil" in Russian. It is maybe also because his father was a military man that he specialized in drawing military scenes. He was a contributor to *La Vie Parisienne*, *Le Figaro*, and *L'Illustration* and for many years he delighted children with his series in *Le Journal du Lundi*.

Always in the military vein, he produced in 1887, for the inauguration of the Chat Noir shadow theater, an immensely successful Napoleonic epic which was followed by others at the Théâtre d'Application. His two known posters, "Expositon Franco-Russe" and "Va t'en guerre," also depict the military. Hence his card for the "Collection of One Hundred" is rather an exception in his work, and although the subject is a civilian he is nevertheless in uniform: the jockey's tunic. To give the impression of speed and motion he lets the jockey and his mount, as well as their shadow, go beyond the line that frames the racetrack. The facial expression of the rider makes his effort and the excitement of the race come alive.

27–38. ALPHONSE MUCHA (1860–1939).

The importance of Mucha is such that currently people speak of a "Mucha style" to evoke the Art Nouveau style. He became well known because of his posters for Sarah Bernhardt. (The First, Gismonda, dates back to Christmas of 1894). He was in charge of advertising for the biggest French industrialists: cigarette paper Job, Lefèvre Utile biscuits, the printer Champenois, bicycles, producers of Champagne and other alcoholic beverages. For these different brands he produced not only posters but also trademarks, calendars and labels. In addition to his production for advertising he also created an abundant oeuvre as a decorative artist: this includes lithographs, but also book illustrations, decorative figurines, textile and jewelry designs and a substantial number of postcards.

His postcards are more often than not reproductions of decorative panels which he produced in large quantities (the four seasons, precious stones, flowers, the arts, etc. . .) or advertising work as noted above. The exhaustive list of this production has been drawn up by Joëlle and Gérard Neudin in their international postcard catalog for 1978. They list at least 162 of which 105 were produced in France and 57 in Czechoslovakia, where he returned quite early in his life. During his French period, at least seven series of "artistic postcards" were published by Champenois, including the most famous series on the months which we reproduce here. All the characteristics of his style are there, the woman with the well developed hair draped in a garment with subtle folds and waves, surrounded by the flora of France which became one of the principal subjects of his studies.

39. C. HENRIDA.

The spirited circle dance of young girls in the forest is a theme often used by Art Nouveau artists inspired by symbolism. Zumbusch used it in a poster for the German magazine *Jugend*, Bistolfi exploited it in 1902 to announce Turin's International Exhibition. The same theme, on a postcard, is by Henrida, an artist about whom we know nothing. This card is number 28 in the "Collection of One Hundred". As always in this type of scene, the girls are warm and light blobs of yellow, red and orange, in contrast to the cold blue and green of the forest.

40. A. CADIOU.

Cadiou has not left more of a trace in the history of art than Henrida. Like him, he executed a card for the Collection of One Hundred which is also of a similar inspiration. This woman with the elongated profile, her long hair spread out, is archetypical of the canons of symbolism. A pink sea, empty and without a ripple, blends in with the sky and serves as the background of the composition. Painted by means of short strokes, this card, from which a dreamlike atmosphere emanates, is, in our opinion, one of the most beautiful of the collection.

41–42. HENRI MEUNIER (1873–1922).

The gravity which emanates from these two cards is quite typical of Henri Meunier's style, and so are his flat colored surfaces and the vigorous contour, particularly card 42, "Sorrow." It is not surprising that this multi-talented artist tried his hand at creating postcards for the publisher Dietrich, for whom he executed a famous poster in 1898. That poster, as well as the Isaiah Quartet (1895), Starlight Soap (1899), or the poster for the Cyclodrome (1900), are among the masterpieces of the Belgian poster. In every endeavor he tackled—he worked as an engraver, bookbinder as well as illustrator—he was flawless, serious, and synthetic, never carried away by the customary exuberances of floral art.

43–46. GISBERT COMBAZ (1869–1941).

Professor of decorative composition and art history, famous orientalist, lawyer, painter and posterist, Combaz was one of the true believers in Art Nouveau, a truly protean talent among the best in Belgium at the end of the 19th century.

As a posterist (La Toison d'Or, "The Golden Fleece," 1895; Ier congrès des Avocats, "First Lawyers' Congress," 1897) he worked mainly for La Libre Esthetique where he exhibited regularly from 1897 to 1914. The influence of the Japanese Ukiyo-e engraving is obvious in the work of this fervent orientalist: his lively colors applied in flat surfaces, often doubly contoured, his nervous arabesques can be found again and again in the several series of postcards which he created (Sailors, Elements, Proverbs).

These four dazzling cards belong to a series devoted to the elements. Beyond the form one notices in the card "L'eau" ("Water"; 46) a Japanese reminiscence; thus it becomes a brilliant adaptation of Hokusai's "Wave".

47–48. VICTOR MIGNOT (1872–1944).

Victor Mignot was essentially a sports illustrator. He started his career at the newspaper Cyclisme belge and then, in Brussels as well as Paris, he worked for a great number of newspapers, especially Le Petit bleu. From 1895 on he executed posters for diverse movements as well as products (Le Sillon, La Libre Critique, Champagne Berton, the Verdussen art posters), but also for the sport of cycling (Cyclodrome 1898, 5th Salon of the Cycle 1897) and for a number of bicycle manufacturers (Cycles Léon Maus, Record Cycles). It is not surprising then, that this series of his postcards, published by Dietrich, is devoted to sport. With a well contoured design, an elaborate composition, carefully divided into a hierarchy of planes, he describes with humor the pleasures of physical exercise. The original frames for these compositions are very "Art Nouveau" but are rather uncommon to his work.

49–50. ADOLFO HOHENSTEIN (1854–?).

From 1889 on, Hohenstein was one of publisher Ricordi's regular designers. He contributed also to the magazine Emporium. He is the author of very many posters of an extraordinary opulence which must be counted among the masterpieces of European Art Nouveau (Dover-Ostend Line; Monowatt; the jeweler Calderoni; Cintura Galliano, 1899; Tosca, 1899; Pigeon shoot, Monte-Carlo, 1900).

For the 1901 International Education and Sport Exhibition in Milan he created a marvel of a poster, which is also used as the cover for a series of cards. Despite the half tones which detract from the sharpness of the line, they give us an idea of Hohenstein's extraordinary talent for composition and color. Hohenstein's trail, after 1906, has been lost.

51–52. GIOVANNI MATALONI.

Mataloni was one of the first great Italian posterists. Practically no biographical information about him is available except that he worked for Ricordi, the great publisher, who inspired the most beautiful creations of Italian Art Nouveau. We are indebted to him for La Tribuna (1897), Festa di Cervara (1904), Pilole ricostituenti Grocio, and many others.

Together with "Madame Butterfly", Puccini's greatest success in 1900 was "Tosca," adapted from a work by Victorien Sardou. Hohenstein and Metlicovitz (two other artists in the Ricordi stable) produced the posters; Mataloni executed a series of 12 postcards. Here he demonstrates brilliantly his skill in composition: he is able to find the setting and the decorative elements which blend with the happenings (plots, arrests, executions) which stud the drama.

53. LEOPOLDO METLICOVITZ (1868–1944).
54. ADOLFO HOHENSTEIN (1854–?).

Though the opera "Iris" has not left a deep impression on the history of music, it has made up for this lack with an abundant iconography. The poster, executed by Hohenstein, is one of only a few designs which can be compared, without detriment, to Mucha's best production for Sarah Bernhardt. As for the series of cards published by Ricordi at the time the opera was staged, they bear the prestigious signatures of Hohenstein and Metlicovitz. The latter advertising artist was as prolific as he was talented (La Tribune, 1897; Brunate Exhibition, 1904; Incandescent Gas Light, 1895). It was he who won the first prize for posters at the Milan Exhibition of 1906 for his placard for the inauguration of the Simplon Tunnel.

The two postcards reproduced in this book are of great quality. In our opinion, Metlicovitz's is more successful than the other card because of the vigor and the originality of the composition. The image of the dead woman cut up into sections, topped by a blood-spattered iris is shockingly violent.

55–58. BERTELLI.

These four cards of a series of six evoke the "Comedia dell'arte" and are signed by an artist for whom we do not have any biographical information. They are truly superb: the character is represented vertically as if cut out of a theater scene. Only his head emerges in the foreground of a horizontal view of an Italian city to which he is linked.

Harlequin (55) dressed in rags symbolized by the multi-colored pieces of his costume, his face covered with a hideous mask, armed with a juggler's bat, is a hilarious, absentminded naive knave; he comes from the valleys surrounding Bergamo.

Pantalone (56) is a typically Venetian name—Saint Pantaleone even has his parish there. He embodies the rich merchant, a cantankerous old man opposed to the servants—Harlequin, Brighella, Pulcinella—in the tragicomic duos in the tradition of the comedy.

Pulcinella, (57) with his large white tunic and his black bird's beak mask is the Neapolitan version of the valet. The doctor's mask (58) corresponds to the pedant's in the farce. He is a native of Bologna, inspired by the character of a lawyer of that city.

59–60. JOHN HASSALL (1868–1948).

Although he may have considered himself a painter (he came to the Académie Julian in Paris to attend Bouguereau's courses), John Hassall is known to posterity as a cartoonist (he contributed to the *Daily Telegraph* and *Punch*), and especially as a posterist. He executed nearly 600 placards, mainly for the theater, printed by David Allen and Sons (The Shop Girl, Little Bo Peep, Cinderella, the Geisha, Orlando Dando, etc.). He was an illustrator of children's books as well and, just like Cecil Aldin, he produced several postcards. These two small boys, taken from "Hassall's Highlanders: Six Comic Types" published by Sands of London are two good examples of his style.

61–62. A.K. MACDONALD.

These two postcards belong to a series signed by an author whom we don't know. They are a reflection of the sophisticated life in London during the splendors of the Victorian age. The many elegant meeting places of these women of London—the theater, the walk along Bond Street, the drawing rooms—are used as pretexts for finely printed, tastefully colored cards which exhale the exquisite refinement of these bygone times.

63–66. IVAN BILIBINE (1876–1942).

After studying law, Bilibine traveled in Switzerland and Italy, and did drawings for a while in Munich. Back in Russia, he worked from 1898 until 1904 with Repine. Connected with the "World of Art" group directed by Diaghilev, he produced for him the decor for the performance of Boris Godunov at the Paris Opéra. After having emigrated and settled in France—where he designed decor for the Russian operas at the Théâtre des Champs-Elysées —he acquired Soviet citizenship and returned to his native Russia.

His style is a transposition of traditional Russian art, notably that of the icon. He is generally very much preoccupied with decorative motifs. His illustrations for *Popular Russian Tales* (1902) are a masterpiece of the genre.

The cards we selected are of the same workmanship. Number 63 is taken from the "Heroes" series (1909): Sadko, hero of the hanseatic city of Novgorod, salutes the city upon his return from a trip. Card number 64, lithographed by Iline, is quite typical of his search for traditional Russian decorative elements. The last two cards from 1904 are two beautiful landscapes, one of the village of Kemsk in the region of Arkhangelsk, the other of Velikij Ustjug.

67–70. PROSPER-ALPHONSE ISAAC.

These four cards, in spite of appearances, have been created by a Frenchman.

The arts of Japan appeared on the European scene from 1855 on. Collected by a circle of ardent enthusiasts (Braquemont, Edmond and Jules Goncourt in France, Whistell in London) they soon had a considerable influence on western art, notably on the painters of the Nabi group.

Prosper Alphonse Isaac was one of the imitators of the color wood engraving in the Japanese manner. He quickly mastered the media and these four cards, taken from a series of seven produced in 1905, are proof of his skill. We may easily be confounded by the artist's skillfulness.

71. DON MIGUEL UTRILLO (1862–1934).

Painter, archeologist and engineer, Utrillo was also a great traveller. He lived for a time in Paris where he adopted Suzanne Valadon's son, the famous painter of Montmartre, Maurice Utrillo. There he also discovered a number of artists who had a great influence on him: Puvis de Chavanne and the symbolists, the Art Nouveau painters Mucha and Beardsley, the pre-Raphaelites. He created several series of postcards, including "Carmen" and "Women," from which our sample comes. It is skillfully divided into two superimposed planes: first the dancer wrapped in her shawl, then the guitarist and singer on a colored background. The entire bottom part of the composition uses the white paper exclusively to represent the dress and the shoes: it is only on the level of the musicians, as if their music had infused it with life, that color appears.

72. J. LLIMONA.

Barcelona had an important publisher of illustrated postcards, Thomas, who gave commissions to Utrillo, Casas, de Cidon and many other Catalan artists. The card we reproduce is taken from a series of ten commemorative cards which celebrate the 50th anniversary of the proclamation of the dogma of the Immaculate Conception, entitled "Ave Maria Purissima". The neoclassical treatment of the subject does not require any special commentary. (At least one card adds, to this otherwise profane and futile album, the religious tone that was lacking.)

73–76, 79. KOLOMAN MOSER (1868–1918).

Vienna, where the postcard was born, was—with Philipp and Kramer and the Wiener Werkstätte which Percy Hacker, described in *The Poster* of December 1899 as "undoubtedly producing the most artistic postcards in the world"—one of the most prolific centers of illustrated postcard publishing. In fact, the members of the Secession (Jank, Kokoschka, Moser, etc . . .) designed hundreds of cards. In the cards we are reproducing, Koloman Moser's presence is preponderant. We find his monogram on numbers 75 and 79, and on 73 his is next to Kainradl's. A key personality of the Viennese movement, he was a member, in turn, of the Club of 7, the Künstlerhaus, from 1896 on, co-founder of the Secession in 1897, and later of the Wiener Werkstätte. Because of the colors—red, brown and gold—as well as the rigid and serious composition, these cards contrast sharply with the arabesques of French or Italian floral art. We should particularly underscore that the vegetation, instead of being developed to excess, is simplified and stylized. This quest, which is typical of the Viennese Secession, makes these cards, which were published in series of ten, masterpieces of the genre.

77. WINIBALD DEININGER.
78. G. LIBERALI.

These two Viennese cards, with two small signatures, are of an exceptional graphic quality.

Deininger paints a highly audacious ballroom scene: the dancer's face is hidden by the hair of his partner who is only seen from the back. By means of this skillful staging he materializes the spell of the dance which lets the couple escape from everything that surround it, even a row of spectators that limits the field of

vision to the top (this is the same process Lautrec used in his poster for the Moulin Rouge). The strangeness of the scene is accentuated by the red of the dancer's hair which only a contour line separates from the background. The illustration is contained in a rectangle at the bottom of which the artist, by means of a few sinuous lines, depicts a harp and a woman's face from which a melody escapes which, in the most classical Art Nouveau spirit, transforms into a spiral only to lose itself in the infinite.

Liberali's "Lieben Leben" represents in the middle of a forest of intricately tangled stalks a cupid, holding a rose and a heart in his hands, standing on a ground that is strewn with hearts. The richness and the opulence of the design make one think of the luxuriance of French floral art. In the frieze on top of the composition we notice the stylization which is so particular to the Viennese Secession.

In addition to the originality of the composition, these two cards have in common a remarkable use of the blank space (the virgin paper) which organizes space so that only two colors in addition to the black are sufficient to fill it.

80–82. CARL JOZSA.

Be they the Graces of the Greco-Roman antiquity (80) or contemporary beauties (81, 82), women were, at the turn of the century, as always, the prime inspiration of artists. Graphic artists such as the Viennese Carl Jozsa could easily respond to the publishers' requests for such pictures. They supplied many variations on this eternal and inexhaustible theme. In Jozsa's series of cards, "Sirenes and Circes," we find again the archetype of the art of the time: unfurled, supernatural hair (80), intricate compositions accentuated by whiplash lines and, as a result of a harmonious color scheme, adorable, vividly contoured faces. Cards 81 and 82 are charming. In the first, we are attracted by the elegant woman's eyes, which blend in perfectly with the rest of her outfit; in the second, the red lipstick (which is in sensuous opposition to the black of her hair) is in a harmonious relationship with the red of the heart she is contemplating—is it ours?

83–94. RAPHAEL KIRCHNER (1876–1917).

Illustrator and contributor to graphic magazines, Raphael Kirchner was one of the most prolific designers of postcards of his time. In addition to the series which he signed, a great number of anonymous cards are attributed to him, although it seems that some of them were created by his wife who also served as his model. We are reproducing three groups of cards taken from three series of cards which we believe are representative of his entire production.

"Vieux temps" ("Old times," 87–90) is an example of his mythological inspiration which he developed in several groups of ten or twelve cards including, for instance, "Leda," "Greek Girls," "Roma" or "In the Seraglio." The series of "Women in the Sun," (83–86) a model of composition, charm and harmony, is one of many variations on the theme of the woman as a "Tender Fruit," "Perfumes," or "Semi-virgin". The last series, from his later period, is a charming evocation of mundane life in Vienna throughout the seasons (91–94). In his entire work this genius of composition remains constant, supported by an always vivid imagination. Within the limited setting which was imposed upon him, he succeeded by means of a thousand ruses and inventions never to repeat himself. He divides the card in every direction, outlines his own frame or moves from a center outward. He is in addition a very able draftsman, be it in black/white or in color. If we compare his work with that of the other great creators of postcards, including Mucha, then we must salute him as the artist who has gone beyond the seeming possibilities offered by the format.

95–96. LEAL DE CAMARA (1877–1948).

The bicycle was in great vogue at the end of the last century. Hundreds of manufacturers opened shop. In France, newspapers like *Le Vélo* (*"The Cycle"*) as well as brands of aperitifs named "Le Vélo" and "Bécane" (Bicycle) —for which Vuillard produced his only poster— prospered. It was the time when Lautrec used to go to the Buffalo cycle-racing track to find his friend Tristan Bernard who was the director. Many were the artists who immortalized "la petite reine" ("the little queen", the nickname of a bicycle at that time) in its hours of glory. Leal de Camara, who contributed to *L'Assiette au beurre* and numerous other publications, did his share before returning to Spain and Portugal. His style is impregnated with the lessons of "Japonism" and the spirt of the Nabi painters. Against a flat colored background, the well contoured color spots of his figures stand out vividly. In a scene like the one of the couple with the tandem bicycle (95), the light emanates from the woman's white blouse. This is in accordance with the purest Impressionist principles. In the card for the bicycle race (96), he applies the Japanese composition technique (with the crowd recessed into the field at the top of the page). To that he adds a humor that is never vulgar and always full of tenderness. Of course, these two cards were taken from a series devoted to the bicycle.

97–98. (ANONYMOUS).

These two German cards also evoke the bicycle. The style and the means used are very different from the preceding ones. Three colors —a yellow, a blue and a black—sparingly used, fill the space while the white of the paper remains dominant. The rather stiff figures are treated with a chromatic naivete which, moreover, is not without charm. Compared with Camara's cards they show clearly the difference between two worlds: one marked by the avant-garde movements (notably the Nabis), the other infused with the atmosphere of popular imagery.

99–102. FERNAND FERNEL.

A regular contributor to the magazine *Le Rire* from 1898 to 1908, Fernel created several posters (Georges Richard Cycles, 1896; Belle Jardinière, 1897; Chicory Bonne Cafetiere, 1897, etc.) and several series of postcards on sports, a whimsical evocation of the cake-walk, and ten cards under the heading "Courses automobiles" ("Car Races"). On the packet the heading is in three languages—French, English, and German—proof of the international circulation of these illustrated postcards. Although I am not a historian of the automobile, we have done some research in order to "place" these racing cars.

Card number 100 undeniably represents in the foreground a Renault and next to it a Mors, the way they competed in 1903 in a Paris to Madrid race (Marcel Renault lost his life in this race).

In card number 101, the car in the middle seems to be a Napier of a type which, with Gabriel at the wheel, won the third Gordon-Bennett Cup in 1902.

Finally, card number 102 represents, again, the Mors at full speed, winning the Paris-Madrid race in 1903. This permits us to date these cards from 1903–1904.

The black background which Fernel intentionally uses makes the cars stand out and intensifies the idea of speed. He presents these race cars from diverse angles, angles which could be called "cinematographic": card number 101 is a clear example of this type and seems to be taken from a film.

103–104. LEAL DE CAMARA (1877–1948).

Camara, whose bicycle postcards were previously noted (95–96), was also a willing painter of the automobile. His issue of the magazine *L'Assiette au beurre*, entirely devoted to careless drivers, is full of gripping movement. In this series of cards he returns to the theme with the same intentionally ferocious humor. His designs are always well covered with color and have a white spot (the sailor's hat and the cloud of dust) which serves as a focal point. The young boy could well be a playmate of the young girls Bonnard liked to paint.

Card 103 has the line "L'enfance de l'automobile ou l'automobile de l'enfance," (The infancy of the automobile or the automobile of the infant) while the caption on card 104 has the driver, about to go off the cliff, announce "Il faut être prudent, mettons en troisième vitesse." (We must be careful; let's put it in third gear).

105. PAUL BERTHON (1848–1909).

A disciple of Grasset, Berthon executed posters which reflect his master's style (Salon des cent, 1895; L'Ermitage, 1897; Lyane de Pougy and Livre de Megda, 1898). Naturally, he used a woman with long hair surrounded by flowers. His originality stems from his autumnal palette where yellows, greens and browns blend harmoniously. These same colors are also to be found in his decorative prints of landscapes and his series of contemporary celebrities, notably Sarah Bernhardt, the Prince of Wales and Queen Wilhelmina (which exists in at least two scales of colors). It is this lithograph, reduced to the size of a postcard, that is here reproduced. The rights to it were visibly acquired by the Dutch publisher Van de Ven. In the United States, the Wilhelmine Chocolate Company did not bother with such precautions and used the same design for advertisements printed in 1903–1904.

106. RAPHAEL KIRCHNER (1876–1917).

This card from a series of 12 is generally attributed to Kirchner. It possesses all the characteristics of his style: skillful composition that makes the image stand out as if it were on a screen, and a surprisingly sparing use of strokes and color to construct a charming Japanese style tableau.

107–108. LÉOPOLD LELÉE (1872–?).

Lelée is best known as a painter of the Provence where he settled, in Arles. There he illustrated such works as Paul Arène's *Stories and Tales from Provence* (1936) and René Barbier's *Blood of the Camargue* (1936). During his youth in Paris, where he studied at the School for Decorative Arts, he produced strange works such as a poster for the Folies Bergère that is full of surrealist elements, and this hand-colored series of ten postcards on the eyes.

Two of the ten charming faces which he painted in the Art Nouveau manner, the arabesques of the hair and the opening up of the flowers are shown against a background of mysterious and disquieting eyes. In the foreground, to complete these strange pictures, is a gigantic eye whose pupil is a flower which watches us. These ten compositions, as well as the poster we mentioned, are unique examples of the presence of the fantastic in floral art.

109–110. (ANONYMOUS).

These two German postcards are very characteristic of Art Nouveau. Mucha's influence is quite evident here (number 109 cannot

fail but to make us think of Sarah Bernhardt's portrait for *La Plume*), but the broadly unfurled hair, the decor and the vegetation are of a stiffness that is far from the master's sensuous compositions! These two busts of women against a roughly tinted green background exist in numerous variations, with larger or smaller sized portraits, in a horizontal as well as vertical format. They are part of the many models which the German publishers, the undisputed masters of the lithographed postcard, exported throughout the world.

111, 114. EVA DANIELL.

With Eva Daniell (we know very little about her), we take up one of the highlights of the illustrated postcard and certainly the best of the very prolific production of the publisher Raphael Tuck. With a remarkable sense of composition and prodigious luxuriance (particularly in card 114), she has left us a handful of small masterpieces which have also been used as designs for menu covers. Nowadays, collectors are vying with one another to acquire these works.

112. ELISABETH SONREL (1874–1951).

A student of Jules Lefèvre, she settled for good in Sceaux in 1895. Very much influenced by the pre-Raphaelites, she created at the turn of the century many mystic and symbolic subjects. This graceful card dates from this period of her work, and it is one of the most harmonious Art Nouveau creations known to us. This young woman, her hair loosened, framed by a skillful composition of water lilies and irises, may serve as a model of the period's art.

113. (ANONYMOUS).

This anonymous German card, "The Sense of Touch," is part of a series on the five senses. It may be interesting to compare it to the preceding one which, although on a related subject, has received different treatment. Executed with a clumsiness that borders on naivete, this young woman contrasts strongly with Sonrel's stylized elegance and sinks to the level of a mere anecdote. Her dress and the surrounding nature are also very awkward. It is a good example of the hundreds of cards produced by minor artists which were available in profusion at the time.

115. (ANONYMOUS).
116. F. DOCKER, JR.

These two cards, one published by Raphael Tuck and distributed in England and the United States, the other published by Raphael Neuber in Vienna, signed "F. Döcker Jr.", seem to us indispensable to complete this album. They illustrate the affectation of style to which the evocation of antiquity and the use of floral art had led some minor artists. Far from the great masters, far even from the vigor of some of their disciples, many artists practiced a mercenary Art Nouveau. Some people may find these two cards charming; we, on the other hand, included them because of their mawkishness.

117–118. (ANONYMOUS).

These two anonymous Viennese cards belong to the numerous series of sketches of fashionable living at the beginning of the century. Number 117 depicts a devotee of the races, elegantly dressed in an outfit with a floral pattern. In the same series, and always elegantly dressed, she is shown at the Prater, at a ball, in a park etc. . .

At the edge of the cold, blue night, her neighbor, enticing and desirable, seems to invite us to join her in the rectangle of warm, yellow light of her quarters. This remarkable setting and the harmony of the colors make this a particularly spellbinding composition.

119. "M.C.".

This card, signed with an unknown monogram, is a small masterpiece. The harmony of the brown and green colors, the wide contour which in a few vivid strokes evokes the landscape, the diagonal composition, the use of the virgin paper to represent the sky and the muff, all this is as admirable as it is uncommon. As we have seen, Raphael Tuck & Sons produced the best (111, 114) as well as the worst (115). That isn't even surprising for a company of its size. From 1871 on, tens of thousands of different models were put into circulation under the easel and palette trademark. In 1903, a competition organized by the company was won by a collector who had no less than 20,000 of these cards. Established all over the world—in New York from 1900 on and in France where they used the slogan "Un mot a la poste"—the production (most often printed in German) of the company remains unequaled in terms of quantity as well as variety.

120. "J".

This second Anglo-Saxon postcard also bears an unknown monogram. The card is taken from a series of ten representing stained glass windows. The art of the stained glass window entered into an important period of renewal because of the Art Nouveau artists' admiration for the Middle Ages. These cards are the only ones we know that refer to that time in history.

121–122. ALPHONSE MUCHA (1860–1939).

These two cards, Emerald and Topaz, belong to the series "Stones", one of many groups of four decorative compositions of a long rectangular format which Mucha executed for Champenois and which were later printed as postcards. This explains why the design does not cover the total surface of the card. The salient features of Mucha's style are all here: the background in the form of a rosette is reminiscent of Byzantine mosaics, a sensuous woman, always of the same type (we have photos from which Mucha worked and they represent his favored models), languishes amidst the flora which invades the lower part of the composition. The whole reflects Mucha's usual mastery.

123–126. (ANONYMOUS).

If Japan influenced western art of late 19th century, upsetting the traditional rules of composition, model and color, so Japanese society opened its doors to the techniques of the western industrial societies. They, too, produced postcards, and we are well acquainted with a series published by Kobunkan in Tokyo. In terms of style as well as subject the cards are graphically in the Japanese tradition. The four cards—out of a series of twelve—shown here illustrate this production to perfection. The manner in which space is used is remarkable, as for instance in card number 123 where the artist brings into view a group of people with parasols, leaving the left side empty, thus giving the impression of motion. These pictures of Japanese life—a caravan under the snow, archers, strollers or Sumo wrestlers—represent a people on the move, anchored in tradition but receptive to all new techniques.

127. ALPHONSE MUCHA (1860–1939).
128. (ANONYMOUS).

We wanted to bring this album to a close with a little confrontation, by comparing two cards which, although they are typically Art Nouveau, are nevertheless quite different. One is Mucha's "Rêverie", published by Champenois, the other is an anonymous one published by Raphael Tuck & Sons. (We know that it was published there even though the palette and easel trademark is missing.) As much as Mucha's work is a model of graphic virtuosity, harmony and decorative skill, so the other is clumsy, awkward and naive. With the same elements—a woman, a frieze and some flowers—the results obtained are absolutely different. The production of an entire generation gravitates between these two poles: influenced by masters such as Mucha and Grasset in France, the members of the Viennese or German Secession, hundreds of artists tried their hand at floral art at the turn of the century. They invaded the graphic and decorative arts to the saturation point. These excesses, this poorly designed superabundance brought about a reaction: Art Deco. But that's another story . . . and perhaps another book.

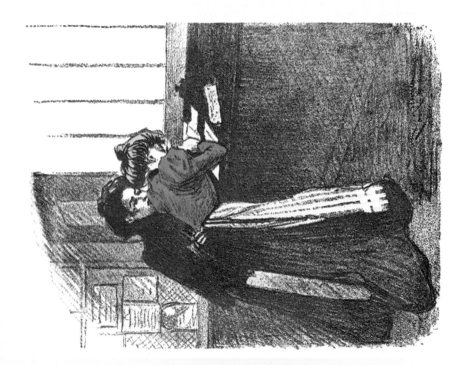

— Mais maintenant Rodolphe... vous aimez bien que Mimi Pinson n'a qu'un bonnet !

J. Villon

J. Villon

14

13

L'EMBOUTEILLAGE

AbelTruchet

Collection des Cent. — E. G. Paris. — J. Chéret.

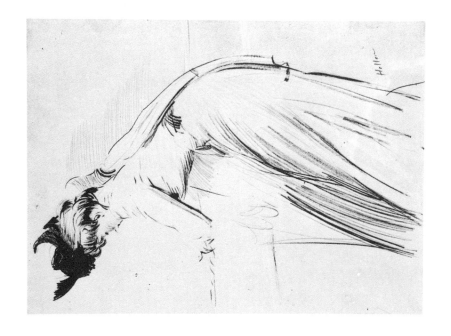

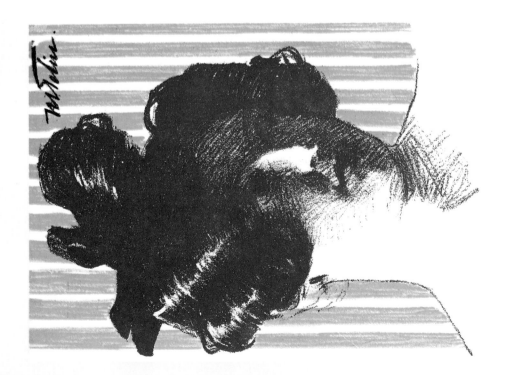

JANVIER

28

FÉVRIER

JUILLET

AOÛT

LA TERRE

LE FEU

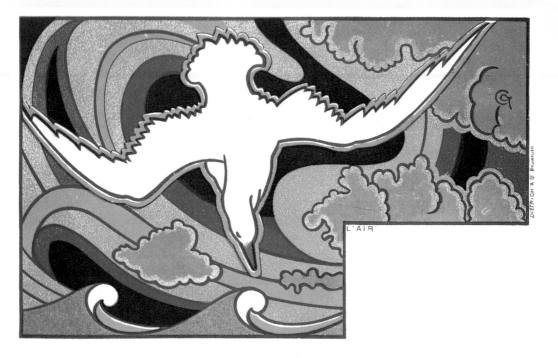

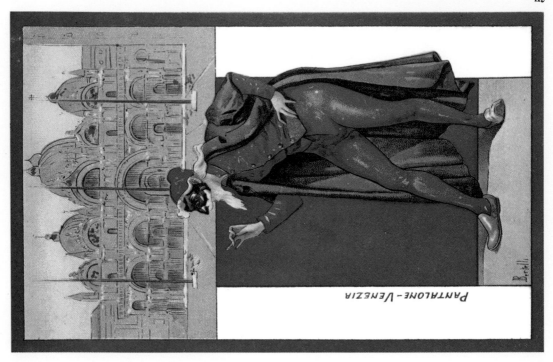

PANTALONE – VENEZIA

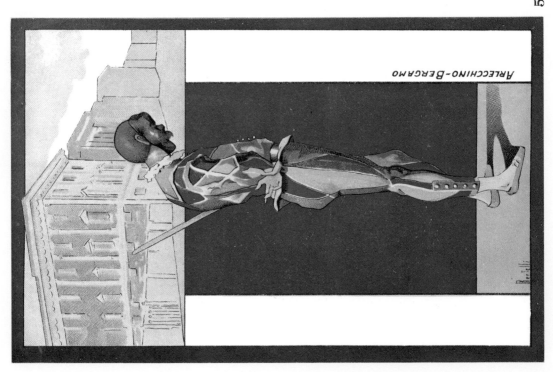

ARLECCHINO – BERGAMO

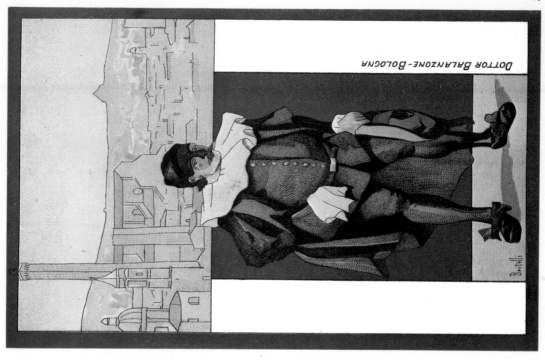

DOTTOR BALANZONE - BOLOGNA

58

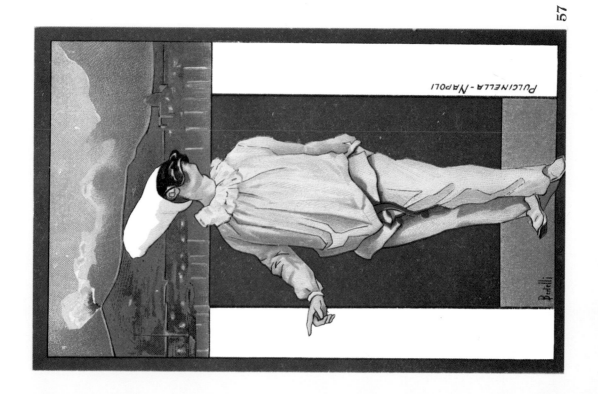

PULCINELLA - NAPOLI

57

MacIntosh.

I'm sweired to bather ye brut

Chisholm.

I'm awfu' gled

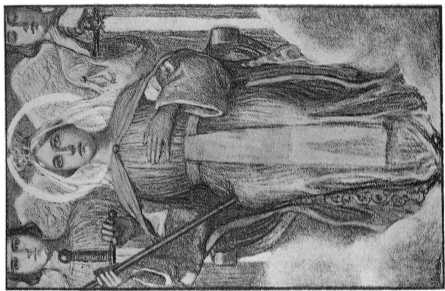

REGINA SANCTORUM OMNIUM

THOMAS — BARCELONA

72

71

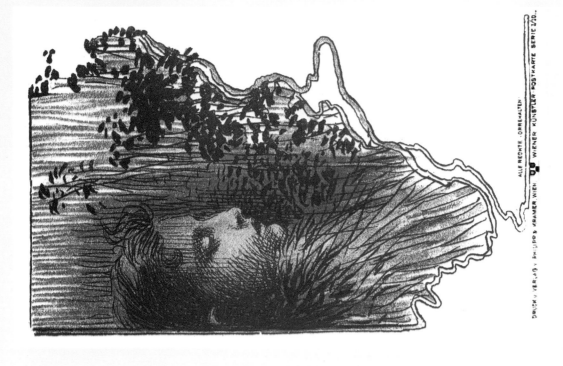

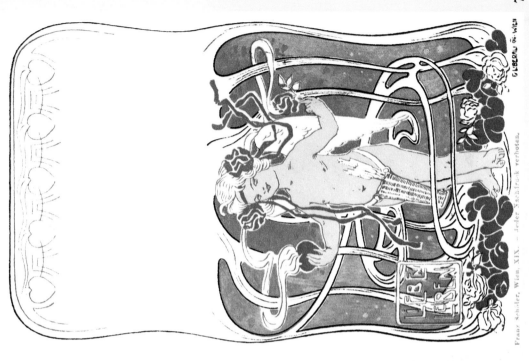

Franz Scholer, Wien, XIX. – Jeder Nachdruck verboten.

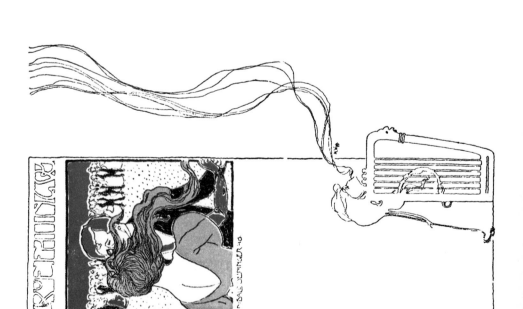

VIEUX.
TEMPS.
• • • ⫶⫶⫶

VIEUX.
TEMPS.
• • • ⫶⫶

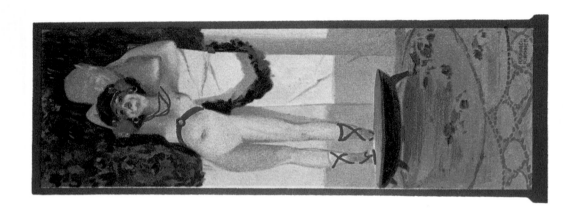

VIEUX. TEMPS. · · · VI.

VIEUX. TEMPS: · · V.

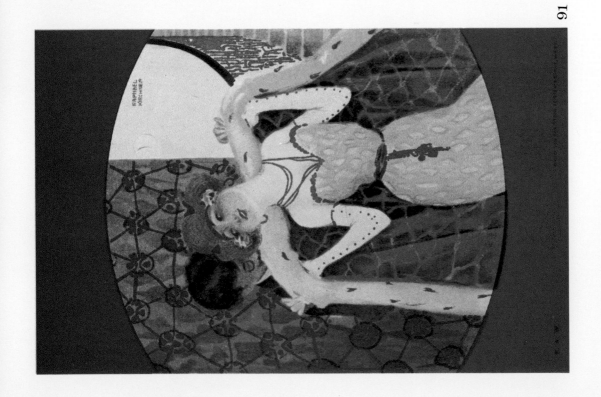

62

61

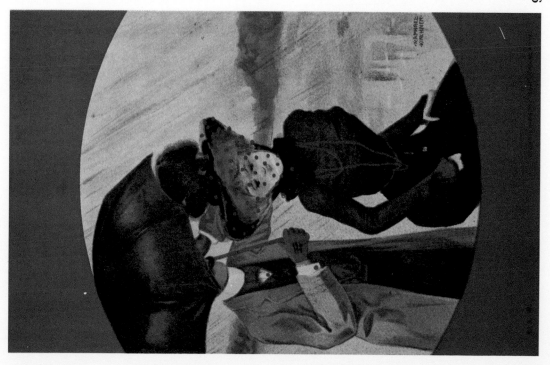

— Il faut être prudent, mettons
en troisième vitesse.

L'enfance de l'automobile ou l'auto-
n. bile de l'enfance.

KONINGIN WILHELMINA

Uitg. J. F. VAN DE VEN, Baarn.

For a Happy Christmas

SERIE 376

E. DÖCKER jun

My hope and heart is with thee.

Tennyson.

E.A.W.

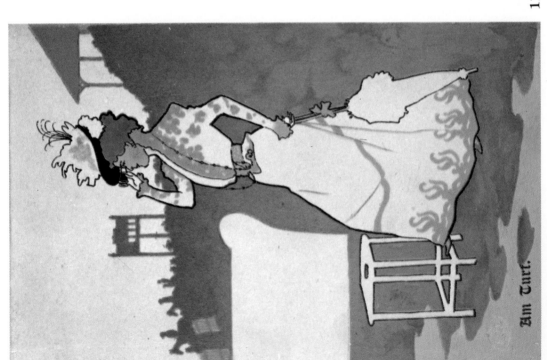

Am Turf.

Late Autumn